Rock Island Press ⚓ Houston, Texas

Anonymous He

a collection of poems
by Louis Skipper

Books by the author

Pip and the Zombies	2010
Teacher's Hands	1993
First Kiss for a New Love	1992
I Hate Green Beans	1992
I Just Want to Dance	1987
Dawn's Song	1985
A Number of Poems	1982

copyright © 2006

Library of Congress Card Number: 2006908604
ISBN: 0-9779859-2-X

Rock Island Press
Houston, Texas
http://www.rock-island-press.com

Love is so short,
* forgetting is so long.*

- Pablo Neruda
(1904-1973)

Contents

Paper Clip Poem 1
Morning Haiku 2
Beach 3
You Said to Call 4
Belize 5
Old 6
The Mowers 7
Yo Pienso En Ti 12
I Think of You 13
When I Close My Eyes 14
Smile 15
He Knows She's There 16
Fever 17
If This Shall Be the Last Time 18
Box 19
Tongues 20
Lump on My Side 21
Afraid to Look 22
Death 23
Bukoswski et al 24
Looking at Oranges 25
Blue Candles, Brass Holders 26
Alone in Deli 27
Poetry 28
The Valentine That I Ain't Got 29
Tuesdays 30
Once 31
Message 32
Beatrice 33
Puppy Love 34
I Think I'll Soon Explode 35
Falling Asleep 36

Morning 37

Old Man Poems 38

Life Ain't No Laboratory 40

Holiday 41

2 AM 42

Missed Flight 43

Christmas '97 44

Cocktail Party 45

Niceman 46

Chinese Take-Out 47

Night Time Fog 48

Son 50

Perhaps 52

They Say 53

Hawk 54

It is Winter in My Soul Today 56

First Day of Summer Vacation 57

Road Trip 58

The Halls of Education 59

You Didn't Notice 60

Where Has Suzy Gone? 62

Otto's Ice House 63

Denise 64

A Reading 65

Teacher's Hands

Harp Player 69

Truck Divers 70

Kittens' Paw/ Waves 72

It Must Have Been Something She Ate 73

The Scent of Her Perfume 74

English Party, 10 PM 75

Little Black Boy 76

I Ask 77

Why? 78

What Would the Neighbors Think? 79

Reaching 80

We Do 82

Haircut 83

Tall in Her Memory 84

In Her House 85

Promises of Picnics 86

James Dean 87

Fried Chicken 88

Christmas in the City 89

A Retelling 90

Teachers Hands 91

He Just Laughs 92

First Kiss for a New Love

Two Blocks of Ice 97

A Good Thing 100

The Shores of Crete 101

If Last Requests Count 103

Construction Worker 104

Tonight I Sleep Alone 105

Once More 106

I Remember When 107

A Relationship 108

Spring and All 109

The Soldier 110

For Terrie 112

For William Carlos Williams 113

Serenity 114

While Fishing 116

Security Guard at 2 AM 117

Silence Gives Consent 118

It's a Long Time Until Monday 120

One Day Follows the Next 121

M & M 122

Turn Off the Lights 125

Anonymous
He

Paper Clip Poem

You fiddled with it in your hands
a paper clip
you bent and twisted
and I thought you were nervous
fidgety
then you opened your hands
and there it was

an apple

Morning –
tiny drops of water
decorate the grass

Beach

He walks along the beach
not bothering to roll his trousers.
As the water washes against his ankles,
he scoops up the wet sand
and lets it sift through his fingers.
In the same way,
he lets time slip away,
sometimes just in a steady stream,
sometimes in clumps and chunks.
Behind him,
the water washes away his footsteps
but it doesn't matter,
there is no one to follow.

You Said to Call

You said to call
so I did.
Your voice was sleepy
on the other end.
I tried to imagine,
and it was not hard,
you curled on the couch
in little sock feet.

Belize
(for Lucia)

In the jungle,
the howler monkeys throw sticks at you.
You climb trees
to escape the wild peccary
and with machetes,
carve a path from one excavation site to another
only to find it grown back by morning.

At breakfast,
you pour hot sauce on your eggs
to make them palatable.
At lunch,
you eat your peanut butter and jelly sandwich
under a tarp as the rain patters above you
and drizzles into puddles around your feet.
At dinner,
you're so hungry,
it doesn't matter that flying bugs fill the air and
land in your soup and on your spoon.

But when the camp is quiet
and night arrives,
you lie in your tent
with his letter in your hand
and you sleep
and smile.

Old

When does a man become old?

Today
Donald Trump said
60 was the new 40.

When I was 28,
I felt 40.
My knees ached, my bones ached,
my body ached.

Now that I'm 40,
I feel like I'm 28.
My body feels strong.
I can play chase and toss
with Coco for hours.

And though I feel young,
I am not,
and sometimes I'm asked for advice, wisdom,
and I surprise myself by having
advice and wisdom to give.

But my heart,
that's what feels old.
It's not my back or my joints
or my feet that hurt.
It's my heart.

The Mowers - I

The mowers have left an uncut patch
where the riders park their bikes in the rack.

The sun is warm when we walk outside
and you take my hand.
Some say your hands are large for a girl
but they fit just right in mine.
And when we hold hands,
you trace your fingers along mine
and up my arm.
When we hold hands,
your hands seldom stay still.
They flutter in mine like a restless bird,
they are delicate
and touch me the lightest touch
and the warm sunshine is not what warms my heart.

The Mowers - II

The mowers have left an uncut patch
where the riders park their bikes in the rack.

You've closed your eyes and are breathing deep
nature's perfume of fresh cut grass.
The warm wind blows your hair and it falls
across your eyes in a way
that, for lack of a better phrase,
thrills me.
Something about it makes you seem carefree
or wild, yes that's it, wild and untamed.
How exotic you are when your hair falls forward
across your eyes,
shading their rich brownness from me,
like a Serengeti cat hiding in the grass.
And when you push it aside
to find me watching you,
you are not surprised.

The Mowers - III

The mowers have left an uncut patch
where the riders park their bikes in the rack.

Your eyes have always held me in their grip.
When the years come between us,
your eyes will be what I remember.
The sun is warm on our skin
and the fresh cut grass tickles us.
You lie next to me,
your hand resting on my chest,
playing with the buttons of my shirt.
Everyday should be like this,
you and I together, my arm around you,
your head on my shoulder,
your sweet cheek touching mine in our embrace.
Your eyes have always sought out mine
and I belong in your eyes.

The Mowers - IV

The mowers have left an uncut patch
where the riders park their bikes in the rack.

There are a few pieces of grass caught in your hair,
your cheeks are flushed,
and I remember what you told me once.
But despite everything we've shared,
each day brings a new goodbye.
Each parting is no indicator
of what the next day will bring.
But like a shared sunset,
we've learned to appreciate
temporal beauty.
If everyday could be Heaven,
we would spend our time together,
but then we wouldn't need this poem
to make the moment last.

The Mowers - V

The mowers have left an uncut patch
where the riders park their bikes in the rack.

I breathe deep nature's perfume of fresh cut grass
and take your hand in mine.
Some say my heart is too big
and my passions too deep
but you navigate the currents of my soul
like a seasoned boatman.
You know where the rough waters are,
where rocks lie hidden beneath the surface,
and you steer through them and make the waters calm.
Lying in the grass and laughing
looking at clouds drifting on the warm wind,
no words needed to communicate,
a simple respite from a hectic life.
Idyllic love, pastoral scene,
the stuff of poems and love songs.

Yo Pienso en Ti

Al amanacer
y por todo el día
yo pienso en ti --
¡Qué recorrimos juntos
y nos amamos uno a otro!
Y a noche,
no me puedo dolmir.
Me pregunto
que tu estás haciendo
y donde tu estas.
Mil mañanas podrán venir,
Mil mañanas podrán pasar
y todavía
yo pienso en ti.

I Think of You

At daybreak
and throughout the day
I think of you –
how we walked together
and loved each other.
And at night
sleep doesn't come.
I wonder
what you are doing
and where you are.
A thousand mornings may come
a thousand tomorrows may pass
and still
I will think of you.

When I Close My Eyes

When I close my eyes
I remember the smell of your hair,
how soft it is against my cheek,
how smoothly it runs through my fingers
and curls at your neck.

When I close my eyes
I remember the fragrance of the skin
of your smooth neck,
how you shiver when I kiss it
and pull you close.

When I close my eyes
I taste again your lips,
how sweet they are
as they press against mine,
how you leave me breathless.

When I close my eyes
I feel your body,
soft and inviting.
I feel your strong arms around me
holding me to you.

When I close my eyes
my heart aches to be with you
to see your face
to look into your eyes
to hear your voice speak my name.

When I look into your eyes.

Smile

How do you expect me to smile
day after day
when day after day
you kill me slowly?
You play with me like a yo-yo,
toying with my emotions,
building me up,
then tearing me down.
What is it that you want from me
that I haven't already offered?

He knows she's there
He hears her voice
the walls are not thick
and it is not his choice
that she is there
while he is here

Fever

Your fever broke sometime during the night –
my lips
upon your cool brow

"If this shall be the last time..."
- Sara Teasdale

If this shall be the last time,
if our paths will not cross again,
then let's make this moment last.

If this shall be the last time
let me linger in your eyes
let me hold you longer
remind me that once I mattered.

If this shall be the last time
stand before me
and let me seal your image in my mind,
for in this parting
a piece of my heart
leaves, too.

If this shall be the last time
let us not speak of it.
Place your hand in mine
and let's laugh and smile
and not think how quickly
time has passed from us.

If this shall be the last time
think not of what we're losing
think not of what will not be
think of what we had
think of me
as I shall think of thee.

Box

What's the box for
he asks
and she places it over her head
peering out of the handle holes
into his eyes

tongues

idle tongues wag –
not like the tails
of petshop window puppies
but like the lashes of a whip
across the back
of a runaway slave

Lump on My Side

For two months
I had a lump on my side
then one day my stool was tan
so I Googled "tan stool"
but had to change it to "tan bowel movement"
because I wasn't looking for furniture.

Afraid to look,
I turn the other way

Death-
    another reason not to love

Bukowski et al

I've not lived a life like Bukowski.
Mine's been free of adventure and excitement,
as if living in only one dimension,
rarely straying from the mundane.
I've not lived a life like Bukowski
and so my poetry lacks such life.
My experiences never vary,
my routine is routine,
my history repeats itself daily.
Emails to friends say
"nothing new here"
even after years.

Looking at Oranges

The grocery stores
are open all night
and every corner
has a 24 hr fast food joint.
He'll always have a place to go.
2 AM comes along
and finds him in the produce section
looking at oranges.

Blue Candles, Brass Holders

I'll never hear Kenny G
without thinking of you
and that's not such a bad thing.
I'll remember our night
of blue candles and brass holders
and…
what can I tell?
The lights were down,
candles lit the room,
and Kenny G played on the stereo.
That is all.

Alone in Deli

In the grocery store
it's noon maybe one.
Young men and their wives
buy groceries –
they pick up fruit
squeezing
smelling
considering.
They buy fresh cut meats
and cans of beans and soup,
loaves of bread.
It's Sunday
and he sits alone in the deli
eating cold chicken strips
and mushy broccoli.
The attendant smiles at him
but it is a vacant smile
saved for lonely customers
who want to feel welcome.

Poetry

Why is this "poetry"
my brother asked.

He said,
On the radio, Keillor read this poem.
It was like,
"I walk to the car
and check the weather
as I get ready to drive to work.
I open the door
and put a bag of DVDs on the passenger seat.
I close the door,
walk around to the driver's side,
climb in, adjust the air, turn on the radio,
and drive to work."

Is that a poem, he asked.

It can be.

The Valentine That I Ain't Got

There is a girl I love a lot;
She's the valentine that I ain't got.

She's all I want, she's all I seek
and though it's true we often speak,
my guts still twist into a knot,
cause she's the valentine that I ain't got.

She smiles at me, and I at her
but then my head grows light and my vision blurs.
Her every feature I have not forgot
cause she's the valentine that I ain't got.

I do not know what can be done.
When I'm with her, we have so much fun.
But there are things I wish were not,
cause she's the valentine that I ain't got.

Not a day goes by nor an evening pass
when thoughts of her aren't first and last.
But my every cell is filled with the thought
that she's the valentine that I ain't got.

If one day my wish comes true
I'll spend my days alone with you
and we'll never regret having risked being caught
cause you're now the valentine that I have got.

It's Tuesday
and I love her.

Once
he broke a telephone.

It wasn't enough just to slam down the receiver –
he slammed it down 3 or 4 times
then yanked the cord from the wall,
lifted the phone above his head
holding it high in one hand
then
with all his strength
smashed it against the ground.

Message

You
are the subject of this poem
You
are its life
its pulse
You
are the blood that flows through it
that gives it life
You
are its essence
without you
this poem becomes meaningless
scratches of ink upon the page
without you
like me
this poem will die

"Beatrice"

One day,
I looked on
a piece of paper
and this is what I saw.
I didn't think
it was your name,
but I couldn't remember
anything else,
so I said it.

You laughed,
and my face
turned red
like the color
of the dress
you wore on Friday.

Puppy Love

He was like a scared puppy
hiding under the porch
too abused to come out into the world again
and be vulnerable,
but she coaxed him out,
lured him with yummy treats
and her sweet voice.
She spoke softly and friendly
and as he crawled forward
she patted his head
and scratched his ears
encouraging him, comforting him,
until finally he emerged into the
sunshine of the world
and she kicked him in his ribs.

I Think I'll Soon Explode

There's a volcano in my soul.
My rage is the lava.
She fuels my anger
and I think I'll soon explode.

I contain it,
try to keep control,
but the fire burns and the fury builds
and I think I'll soon explode.

She melted my heart of ice
with love that took away
the cold death of my winter.
Now my heart is in turmoil.
A witch's cauldron,
it boils and seethes
and the pressure builds and cracks appear
and I think I'll soon explode.

The slopes of the mountain are calm;
there is a breeze, the grass waves.
But the animals know.
They feel the tremors underfoot,
they feel the heat, they sense the steam,
cracks appear,
and I think I'll soon explode.

Falling Asleep

I remember falling asleep
with the phone in my hand
and you on the other end.

I remember it had been another long day at school
    another uncooperative kid
    another memo
    another parent conference

I remember it was late at night
and you'd spent another long day at work
    another customer couldn't be pleased
    another coworker being an ass
    another eight hours on your feet

I don't remember who called whom
or what we talked about
but I remember the days were long
and the nights were short
and all that mattered was who was on the other end.

I remember falling asleep
with the phone in my hand
and when I finally spoke
you had fallen asleep, too.

Morning

It is the morning sunlight
that wakes him
to hear her soft breathing.
He turns toward her,
nestled at his side.
Her face glows smooth,
her skin delicate,
and he's afraid to touch her,
afraid that if he does,
she will crumble
and this dream will break.

Old Man Poems

I was told not to write old man poems.
You're only thirty, he said.
But I'm sitting alone watching TV.
Tonight I did my laundry,
pulled shirts from the hamper
and smelled the scents from each day.
It's a good smell, a fragrant history,
and I think -
Somebody should be here
to smell this cologne with me.
Someone should be here
to watch me pour soap into the machine,
to watch the clothes spin in the drier.
Someone should be here with me
to sit on the counter of this washateria
and talk with me about how the day went.
But I'm alone.

I was told not to write old man poems.
You're only thirty, he said.
But I feel a stiffness in my joints
and at the end of the day my back hurts
and I lie soaking in a warm bath with a book.
When I walk, I hear my knee and hip grinding.
My wrist throbs whenever I put pressure on it.
My vision and hearing slip further into the past.
I find myself driving down the road
wondering what my destination was,
or I'm in the kitchen
or in my study or the closet
and I don't remember why I'm there.

I was told not to write old man poems.
You're only thirty, he said.
But in the evening I sit on the porch alone
where the air is cool
and my stereo plays baroque classics softly.
Pachelbel's Canon in D is my favorite
for a night like this
and though I don't smoke, I think I should.
I think a man sitting alone on his porch
thinking thoughts such as mine
should have a cigarette in his hand
should watch the glow of the tip in the night
but I watch the moon
and tonight it is full and low on the horizon
and there is an emptiness next to me.
A hole where a woman should be
with my arm around her.
A gaping hole in my heart -
I don't think it's the most original thing to say
but it works for me -
a gaping, throbbing, painful hole in my chest
a vacuum sucking in all the pain
of all the sorrows from all the years
on what should be a beautiful, peaceful night
a fall night, Pachelbel, and a full moon
a cool rustling through the leaves
and the sound of cicadas
are all I have for company.

I was told not to write old man poems.
You're only thirty, he said.

Life Ain't No Laboratory

Life ain't no laboratory
where you can put on a long white coat and
carefully measure out different fluids and
chemicals into glass beakers and
apply heat or stir gently and
consult lab manuals
and if it doesn't turn out the way you hoped
you just put it down the sink
make a few notes
and start over
cause there's plenty of time to get it right.
No, life ain't no laboratory.

In life,
you do what you can with what you've got and
hope it doesn't blow up in your face.
Life offers no protective eyewear or
rubber gloves or breathing masks
not even a long white coat to protect your clothes.
You throw things together as you come across them,
cross your fingers and hope it works and
there's no manual and no notes
and what happens, happens.
No, life ain't no laboratory.
You do the best you can and
hope it comes together before time runs out.

In life, there's no room and no time for regrets.
That's why I only have two.

Holiday

The sirens had stopped
but their echo was in my ears.
The lights of the police cars
and emergency vehicles
spun and danced dizzily
across the buildings and people.
Suddenly, it seemed like all the holidays
rolled into one moment.

The lights were Christmas,
and the police and detectives
hunted and lifted
and searched like Easter.
The fireworks were over,
smoke and sulfur still in the air
burning my nostrils.
But most of all Halloween –
the blood,
the blood splattering the walls.

2 AM

The phone rings
and it is 2 AM.
He looks at the clock,
its numbers turning his face a sickly green.
He jumps at the sound
wondering what news could be brought
at 2 AM.

The phone rings,
his stomach twists,
his semi-conscious thoughts
turn to puzzlement
as he searches the sheets next to him.

The phone rings
and his eyes open
to look for her,
to verify what his hands have discovered.

The phone rings
and he sits up,
wondering if she has risen to answer
but the room is still.

The phone rings
and it is 2 AM.
He looks at the nightstand.

The phone rings
and then is silent.

Missed Flight

Finally,
the captain came down the long hallway
laughing at an unheard remark
made by the long-legged stewardess
at his side.
Somewhere,
the music of a harmonica sang a tune
that would have found itself
more at home in a bus station.
A young man in a pressed cotton shirt,
denim walking shorts,
tennis shoes with blue stripes
and hanging in his left hand
a jumble of flowers -
pink and yellow, green,
red, purple,
white.
He wanders through the lobby
looking at faces,
searching empty seats
while,
a thousand miles away,
a reporter writes,

Female, 24, dies in auto accident.

Christmas '97

"Human kind can not bear
    very much reality."
        - T. S. Eliot

Your gifts still wait here
under the Christmas tree –
I haven't the strength to move them.
They hang in the balance –
denying the reality
of what is
and what is not.

Cocktail Party

I
had to tell them
your father was ill
when they asked
where you were
something sudden
you
had to rush to his side

What was
I
supposed to do
tell them
you
had left me
make it real
speaking it like that
having them all
look at me
with
uncomfortable eyes

Niceman

The little children
knock on his door
asking for popsicles,
their fingers
sticky with anticipation.

Sometimes
they remember.
Thank you, niceman,
they say.

Bye, niceman.

Eating Chinese Take-Out
on a Wednesday Night

With a great uproar
the front door swung in,
falling off its hinges,
followed by the police,
a thousand guns drawn.
Looking up,
he asked,
Did you bring the sweet-n-sour?

Night Time Fog

                   "I'm not crying," she said.
Her back was to him,
almost lost in the fading sunlight.
It was a statement.
Spoken as matter-of-factly
as when she had said,
                "I'm leaving you."
                 (She didn't.)
This time those were his words.
He was leaving her,
teetering
like a tightrope walker
on the idea of staying –
falling either way would be bad.
But leaving was something "they"
always did, not him.
He thought he was only doing it
to beat her to the punch.
She had put the idea in his head
when she had come back
from not leaving.
The idea had said,
                "Don't be here when she goes.
                Next time, she might not return."
So he told her,
                "I'm leaving."
She didn't believe him,
so he shoved her away.
Pretty hard.
Some psycho-analyst might say
he was trying to shove away
some deep insecurity of his own,
that the aggression he was exhibiting toward her

was actually aggression he was feeling toward himself,
some internal conflict, struggle,
that he could not resolve
and, thus, had to act out against those he loved.

It's good he's not seeing a psycho-analyst.

They were on the porch
and night time fog
had come in off the lake
when she said,
                    "I'm not crying."
                    "Neither am I."
                        (That's what he said.)
Which brings us to now
where it is midnight
and he is reading the back of a postcard
with a picture of the beach
and a cartoon sun saying
                    Welcome to Florida
and in her delicate hand
she has written,

> *Missing you*
> *wasn't half as hard*
> *as I thought it would be.*

Son

Your clothes are tiny,
miniatures.
Holding them,
I feel like a giant and to you,
perhaps I am.
It seems
at this rate
you will soon catch up to me.
I remember
when you were so small
I could hold you in one hand.
The only clothes you wore then
were t-shirts I couldn't even fit over my head
(and I tried.)
I wore your t-shirt
like a little hat
while walking around the room
bouncing you in my arms.
Those were days
that don't seem long ago,
but today you walk and talk
just like a regular person
(almost.)
Your innocence,
your ability to be amazed by
such simple things as...
as flowers and trees
and the cows in the pasture next to the freeway.
I remember you pointed and yelled moo...

Whatcha doing?

A little voice to turn me from my daydream –

Hey, kiddo!
Just folding the laundry.
Momma's still asleep.

You haul your tiny self into a chair
and then onto the table where you sit –
feet swinging,
shoe laces dangling.

Did you put these on yourself?

I tie your shoes, proud.
Your left shoe is on your left foot,
your right shoe on the right.

Yep!
What are we going to do today?

Your face beaming, exuberant
eyes wide, excited.

I don't know, son.

I say,
lifting you warmly into my arms.

What do you want to do?

Perhaps

She didn't know
he listened
while she
talked to her aunt
about Phil
and how,
on their first date,
he had taken her to a bookstore
and browsed for hours.

It was not her idea of fun.

But now,
she is willing to stand in line
for over an hour and a half
to meet an author
and have a book signed for him.

Perhaps this is love.

They Say

They say you stayed awake last night –
pacing the floor,
sitting, standing.
You were waiting
for what you knew
was also waiting.
They didn't know
your attempts to delay the inevitable.

They say you spoke,
sounding nervous but coherent –
telling stories, telling memories,
even jotting down notes for future writing.
They say this was a positive sign.
They didn't know
your attempts to delay the inevitable.

They say your laugh sounded odd.
They said it might be the medicine.
They would have called
had you said something
or had they known.
I could have been there,
said good bye,
seen you off on your journey.
But there was no more
delaying the inevitable.

Hawk

Cold November morning
grey sky
a strong north wind --
    driving
    down one of those roads
        in South Texas
that are there only
    to get you across an expanse of land
        populated
            by scrubby trees
                rusted oil wells
    and now, an occasional house or two.
        I looked up
    and saw a hawk
hovering on the wind.
                    Some may explain
            that he was eyeing his lunch
        waiting for the right moment
    to dive   and catch
a field mouse squealing in his claws.

Some may propose
    that he was waiting
       for his mate
planning a meeting
    like Whitman's
       "Dalliance of the Eagles."
I believe he hovered there
          because it was fun
    to float in mid-air
moving neither forward nor backward
       to subtly drop a wing
    and slide left or right,
      to tilt them
    and move up or down.
    I believe
   he hovered there
because he was free
   because the sun was warm.
    I believe he hovered there
      because he could.

It Is Winter In My Soul Today

She gives one more reason for pain,
one more cause for hurt,
every thought of her
   is one more twist
     of the knife
       she's shoved
         in his soul.

Slamming doors do no good.
Why does she shut them tight?
What happened to her profession of love?
Like the summer day,
it was killed by the coming of winter.

Who taught her heart's wind to blow so cold?
It comes like a memory
turning his insides to frost.
Her love had melted his heart.
His stone wall, his barricade to pain,
his defenses breached by her love,
only to invade,
   to overthrow
     to kill, to maim,
       to slaughter.

It is winter in my soul today.
What is left?

Feet shackled, arms in chains,
a shuffling last walk to the gallows.

First Day of Summer Vacation

I

hit the snooze bar
hit the snooze bar
hit the snooze bar

I

hit the snooze bar
hit the snooze bar

hit
the snooze bar

hit the snooze bar

I hit the snooze bar

hit the snooze bar
hit the snooze bar

hit the snooze bar
hit the snooze bar
hit the snooze bar

I wake up
and it's noon.

Road Trip

Sleeping in my seat
tired from my long trip
the evening sun shining warm on my face...

eyes long ago grown weary
slowly dropping closed
while the a/c cools me
and the sun warms me
and the classical music lulls me...

too bad I'm driving.

The Halls of Education

He walks the Halls of Education –
Past rooms
behind whose doors
are tomes of wisdom and knowledge.
Past rooms
behind whose doors
are speakers proclaiming, imparting, enlightening.
Past rooms
behind whose doors
are ears and minds that listen,
are future generations,
are our hope for tomorrow.
He walks the Halls of Education
to an office
to complete paperwork on his students –
one caught cheating,
one who dropped out,
one who brought a gun to school to solve his problems.

You Didn't Notice

You didn't notice
today
that I wore new perfume.
You didn't notice
today
when I came in the room.

You didn't notice
today
that I'd redone my hair.
You didn't notice
today.
You just sat in your chair.

You didn't notice
today
that the kids weren't at home.
You didn't notice
today
that I'd been here alone.

You didn't notice
today
that your dinner was warm.
You didn't notice
today
but you didn't mean harm.

You didn't notice
today
how much older I feel.
You didn't notice
today
that my world seems unreal.

You didn't notice
today
the weight of my heart.
You didn't notice
today
I was falling apart.

You didn't notice
today
the lines on my face.
You didn't notice
today
I need an embrace.

"What's that?"
you asked,
a questioning look.
"What's that?"
you asked,
lost in your book.

Where Has Suzy Gone?

From outside,
I can hear the swish
of Papa
smearing plaster over the wall.

Had I been older, I might have asked why?
Had I been bigger, I might have said no.
Had I been stronger, I might have run away.

Instead,
I just stood still
while he nailed boards
over the space in the wall.

Papa said it was a game,
another game.
I never liked his games.

I want to go to the park.
I want a puppy.
I don't like playing Papa's games.

I can't sit down here.
It's dark, and it's dusty.
I hear Papa moving around.
Soon Momma will be home.

I can hear her asking for me.
"Where has Suzy gone?"
And Papa says,
"She has gone to get eggs."

Otto's Ice House

The patrons all touch the waitress.
They touch her waist just below
the black halter top
and just above
her short, black shorts.

She puts her arm on their shoulders
and presses her body up close.
Her red lips speak into the ears
of her customers --
the same red lips that left
their mark on the cigarette
when I sat down.

When she bends over
to pull a beer from the cooler of ice,
the men look at each other
and smile.

Denise

Her name was something like
    Denise or Diane.
He met her at the mall
and from somewhere
found the courage
to ask her out.
Like a cartoon,
his jaw dropped
when she said yes.

He was to meet her
in the food court
after work
on Thursday.

Instead,
he stood behind
a column
and watched her wait.

A Reading

I was there the night Yeutushenko died.
I was sitting on the back row
watching and waiting
and listening to the poetry.
I held the book in my hand.
An hour had passed.
I waited for him to finish,
waiting for his signature.

Then,
at what must have been the grand climax,
he stood at the edge of the stage,
his arms spread wide like Daedelus,
and with one loud exclamation,
teetered,
fell,
and it was over.

Louis Skipper

Teacher's Hands
(1993)

For MRM

Harp Player

I fell in love with a harp player once.
I saw her in a concert,
admired the delicacy
with which she played,
and came up with a metaphor –

She is a spider
weaving a web of music.

The skin on her arms rippled like waves,
the muscles undulated
while the buzz of violins
filled in the spaces around her.

Truck Drivers

The truck drivers pull up
and climb down from their cabs
stretching their backs completely unlike cats
waking in the sunshine.
They stretch a lot like truck drivers
do after a long drive.
Then the wind will blow by and you can smell them.
But there doesn't have to be any wind
because the smell will kinda' creep
up your pants leg or across a table
or something
until it gets close enough to slide
right in your nose.
But they'll be smelling
kinda' like old men smell
when they sit on the porch
of a little store in a small town
up in the hills of Arkansas
with a population of about seventy.
The one old man will be telling some story
that doesn't make any sense
and the other old man is spitting tobacco on the floor
and dribbling it on his chin
and the one armed black man is rolling
a cigarette on his knee.
And then some rumbling truck drives by
with a load of hay and a girl and everyone waves
and one of the old men says
Isn't that the Thompson girl but nobody knows.
That's how the truck drivers smell.

But not all of them.
Some wear cologne
and look like they're going to some club
with flashing lights and
music that thumps all night long
so you can't sleep
and you have to just lie there
until you remember
those squishy yellow ear plugs you got from work
thinking one day you might need them.
So you stick one in one ear
and one in the other
but your blood begins pounding
so you pull 'em out and notice
they've got wax on them and make a mental note
to clean your ears in the morning.
But those truck drivers' hair is all in place
and they've got on cologne
that doesn't smell too bad
and they act like they're going to pick up some girl
who likes truck drivers whose hair
is all in place and wear cologne
that doesn't smell too bad and gold necklaces
and who won't mind doing it in a truck
that needs a ladder to get to the door.

Writing these words
 a kitten's paw
  interferes

Waves crashing on the beach –
 at night their sound frightens him

It Must Have Been
Something She Ate

During the movie
she began to complain
and
by the middle of the show
she felt so bad
he had to take her outside
to breathe cool night air
and sip a cup of water.
It didn't seem to help.
They went home.
She had to lie
in the back seat
with her head resting
in her hands.
At home
he carried her to bed.
By morning
she felt fine,
well-rested.
They sat together in the kitchen
drinking coffee
and to himself,
he wondered how the movie ended.

The Scent of Her Perfume

His hair is sticking up
in that funny way it does
during the winter
when he pulls his sweater over his head
that makes her laugh
and
something faint comes to memory
a slow image
brought on by the slight scent
of her perfume
lingering from last winter

English Party, 10 pm

The apartment is crowded
with the sweet smell of liquor,
loud reggae,
and the voices
of twenty-some people.
They're talking
but I understand
none of it.
I stand against the wall
and listen to the people
and watch their faces.
A drifting fragment of conversation
reaches me and
I step in long enough
to lose interest,
waiting for the conversation
to turn to Frost
or Hemingway.

Little Black Boy

A little black boy
raced his tricycle
down the sidewalk
and waved to me.

"Nicholas!"
His momma yelled.
"Get in here!"

I shrugged
and climbed the steps
to my apartment.

              sitting
     up   in the
     ambu   lance
                    do
                   you
                  have
           a son
           named
            how
            ard

            i ask

Why?

"So,"
he said,
having read her diary.
"You think you're leaving me."

What Would the Neighbors Think?

They must have seen you arrive that morning –
when I ran out the door and greeted you.
I know they saw me lift you
off the ground with a hug.
I wonder what they thought
when I took your overnight bag
from the trunk.
I'm sure they waited until the evening
and they saw me leave
in my creaseless tux
and you in a strapless gown.
I wonder what they thought that night
when the house dimmed to only one light.
If they listened close enough,
they could hear the music
and the laughter.
In the morning,
they knew you were still there,
that you had stayed the night.
Outside,
when I held you for so long
and gave you that kiss
and watched you drive away,
I turned
and could see them looking out
between the curtains.

Reaching for Cookies

You swatted my hand away
like I was a child reaching for cookies.
What did you think I would do? Spoil my appetite?
You've merely whetted it,
given me food for thought.

It's a long road, this life,
and it's a cliché.
We've walked a trail
that's wound past many a scenic view
but has fallen just short of paradise,
stopped short by too many years
of knowing each other.
Stopped short by the line
that divides friends from lovers.

So I test that line.
I want you to be more
than just another source of inspiration
for my poetry.
Before we met the lives we would eventually lead,
we had no idea what direction life would take us.
We could talk about things we didn't intend to do.
We could say and do things
with little concern for the consequences.
We could laugh and dream.
Tomorrow was a time that was always one day away,
but has now arrived.

A day whose hours tick by constantly, quickly,
echoing in the silence
that seems so much a part of the future.
A silence that lies in wait so quietly
that I fear the uncertainties it holds.

I fear death.
Not my own, but of those I love.
I fear the pain of loss.
I fear the pain of losing love.
I fear love.

So I reach out my hand slowly to touch it,
hesitantly, carefully,
like reaching out to pet a dog,
a strange dog, an unfamiliar dog,
wondering if it will lick or bite,
wondering if it will be enemy or friend.

And you swat me away
like I was a child reaching for cookies.

We Do

Sitting in silence, they look at the stars.

I want to be happy and carefree he thinks,
    lying down, looking at her back.

How did we end up here? she thinks
    and turns to look at him.
"Why don't you show me some constellations?"

"You know I don't know that stuff."

"You used to pretend. Remember?"

He remembers.
He remembers how they used to play that game,
lying on their backs, looking at the stars…
They would laugh till tears came to their eyes
making all the lights twinkle like stars,
then roll into each others arms and just lie there.

"Pretend you see a constellation."

"Nobody pretends anymore."

Haircut on the Front Steps of the Music Building at
Howard Payne University, Brownwood, Texas

She had only taken a few snips
with my blue handled scissors
before the man with the video camera arrived
and that night,
before a thousand eyes,
my image
was flashed across a gigantic screen.

I can still feel the caress
of her hand through my hair.

Tall in Her Memory

There you were
tall in my memory –

Walking toward me
is it the distance
I ask

when you are close enough
you reach out

a wrinkled hand

stooped
faltering

In Her House

"See this heart?" I asked,
pointing to the heart
I had carved from
the trunk of a tree
with a chainsaw.
"See this heart?
I made that for her."

"See that swing?" I asked,
pointing to the swing
that hung on the porch
in front of the picture window.
"See that swing?
I bought that for her."

"See this door?" I asked,
showing him how it opened and closed,
smoothly, slowly.
"See this door?
I fixed it for her."

I went all around their house
showing him all that I had given her,
all that I had made and fixed,
until he picked up the baby.

"See this baby?" he asked,
holding their son
just weeks old.
"See this baby?
I made her a *mom*."

Promises of Picnics

I stood in the parking lot watching her drive away. I could taste where her lips had touched mine and still felt her in my arms. We had laughed and loved that evening, and she had made promises I knew she wouldn't keep.

This was not the first time we had been together. We had met five years before. Later, she moved away, then I moved away and now, by chance, we were living in the same town again.

She said the same things now that she had said then, made the same promises. I knew what would happen next. We would see each other twice, maybe three times more. Then her days would get busier, her evenings would become full. She would promise, "Saturday," but something would come up and she would have to cancel. Then she would stop returning my calls.

I know all these things as I walk upstairs to my bedroom and put her phone number on my dresser.

James Dean Killed in Crash
- Los Angeles Examiner, October 1, 1955

Crushed and broken steel hurts his eyes
and he pulls his hand away
from the sharp edges,
bile rising in his throat.
Turning away to breathe deep,
to quell his tumbling stomach,
he coughs at the spilling diesel,
squealing brakes still ripping through his ears.

What if I had died?

Could he have become an icon
of today's rebellious youth?
This plodding accountant
with a permanent slump
who, when walking down streets,
studies the far-from-perfect features
that return his glances
in storefront windows.

Probably not.

This was no Porsche Spyder,
no clump of aluminum,
no dead idol in 1955.
This was a Volvo
with a reinforced frame
and a twisted fender,
an accountant with a sore knee
and a stiff neck
questioning his impact

Fried Chicken

I saw a woman on the side of the road whose sign said:

> jobless homeless
> mother of 2 children

I had to wonder where her kids were at that moment.
Perhaps under an overpass somewhere?

I had two boxes of fried chicken on the seat next to me. They
had been running a special – buy one, get one free. I thought
about shoving one out the window at her, but the light turned
green, and I knew the people behind me were probably in a
hurry to get somewhere themselves, and I had originally
planned to put the extra box in the fridge and eat it the next
day, which I ended up not doing and instead ate them both
that evening while watching some movies I had rented, so I
just drove away and went home.

I forgot about her until I wrote this.

Christmas in the City

It's a small price to pay for love –
twenty dollars.
A warm room, too.
Snow curls at his feet,
tires push slush into the gutter
running next to the street.
In the store window,
his face
flashes green then red
as the lights declare
peace on earth.
Twenty dollars isn't bad
considering all the money spent
on the unsure thing.
Two years lost to the land of memories
and nothing to match the pain,
not even the cold biting his ears.
"Memories are all I have,"
he says out loud.
Sparkling packages walk past.
Cars yell, lights wave.
White Christmas
O Come All Ye Faithful
The First Noel
come drifting out of the sky.
The cold makes him shake
as he opens his wallet.
Blowing mist from his mouth,
he throws twenty dollars to a Santa
whose bell rings *thank you.*

A Retelling

I told one
it happened in the war
when a VC
got in a lucky swipe.

I told another
it happened in the ghetto
when a dozen homeboys jumped me,
one getting me from behind.

Once I said
it happened in the classroom
when an angry student
didn't like his F.

But the truth is,
it happened on the highway
when a young driver
decided to go through me
instead of around me,
leaving a scar on my arm
and a hole in my memory.

Teachers Hands

Sometimes
I wish I was
swinging a hammer again,
putting up a fence,
installing a garbage disposal.
I wake up
wishing all I had to do
was mow a yard,
paint a wall,
fix a broken window.

But yesterday,
while eating fajitas on the porch,
my girlfriend looked at me
and said,

You have teachers hands now.

He Just Laughs

Like a tightrope walker,
he teeters
across the back of the park bench.
He flails his arms for balance
but falls anyway,
laughing.
She laughs, too, as he dusts himself off
but he knows she is impressed.
Dropping to the grass
next to where she sits,
he pushes her back
and kisses her.

It's warm in the park
but she's comfortable
in her flower print dress.
The dress
reminds him of spring.
It makes him think of the wind,
the way it ripples around her body.

He kisses her
and rolls onto his back,
laughing again.
He feels he loves her.
He thinks about this
and notices that she is laughing.
This makes him smile,
to know she is happy.

He finds her enticing
and thinks perhaps it is her hair.
It's rich and brown
and hangs to just above her shoulder.
Something about it reminds him
of a horse's mane.
He decides not to mention this,
not wanting to compare her to a horse.

Instead,
he reaches out
and takes a handful of it
and tugs
and says,
"I love your hair."
He runs his fingers through it
for a little while
then plays with the nape of her neck.

She likes this and smiles
and scoots closer to him.
She rolls onto her side
and pats his stomach
like it was a small drum.

He doesn't know if he likes thinking
that his stomach is like a small drum
but he likes it when she pats it
so he doesn't say anything.

He just laughs.

First Kiss for a New Love
(1992)

for my family

Two Blocks of Ice

Two blocks of ice
sit on the sidewalk
outside an old store,
melting.
It is summer in the Southwest
and, in the distance,
the buildings and trees
squirmed.

Down at the soda shop
the sound of a juke box
and a few feet tapping
wearily makes its way outside
where two guys
stand in the shade
drinking colas and talking.

Dirt
from the shoulder
of the road
swirls in little gusts,
dancing in the sun.
The occasional breeze
runs in across the vacant lot
catching the smell of cut grass,
past the soda shop,
cooling the two guys talking
and carrying their conversation to me.

What are you going to do this summer?

Do I have any options?

The wind shifted
and I looked across at the soda shop.
The two guys
were leaning against the building
trying to keep cool.
As I watched,
they continued talking,
emphasizing with pointing fingers
and gesturing arms.
I couldn't hear them
and finally, they collapsed
back against the wall
and exhaled slowly.
I heard one of them yell,

Bring us another Coke,

and in a bit
a waitress came out
with two sodas.
She must have been about seventeen,
wearing a short skirt
and shorter top.
It was summer
and I guess she didn't mind.
Her legs were nice
and I think one of the guys said,

How's that for an option?

and they laughed.

She gave them their bill
but that breeze came by
and took it from their hands,
tossing it down the street.
A dog chased after it,
jumping
until it disappeared,
then stopped outside the old store
to lap up what was left
of the two blocks of ice.

A Good Thing

"Too much of a good thing, boy,
too much of a good thing...."
He stared at the soles of two dusty boots
propped on the desk in front of him,
the worn boots of a hardened construction worker
he called Dad.
In his sheet metal site office,
the hum of the small window a/c
covered the noise of the work outside.
He stepped over to the window
playing with the memory of her face
and looked down
at the crowd of crumpled coffee cups
that had gathered near the trash can.
He stepped on one,
flattening it with his toe.
Looking out the window once more,
he wiped the dust from his eyes
and cleared his throat.
"It's happened again, Dad."

The Shores of Crete

Greek sailors
fishing off the shores of Crete
laugh at the American women.

The women, in their gaudy clothes,
with their cameras and fantasies,
take pictures of the sailors –
young Greeks with tanned bodies
from days in the hot sun,
muscles tight under their skin
from days of hard work.
Not muscles from the gym at the country club
or tans from hours in the tanning booth.

Greek sailors
fishing off the shores of Crete
laugh at the American women
and their fantasies.
The sailors pull nets of fish on board,
their hands, calloused and cut.
They breathe the smell of fish
that would make the American women cringe.

They are proud of the day's work
and laugh at the American women
who have nothing better to do
than leave their homes
to take pictures of Greek sailors
fishing off the shores of Crete
and fantasize.

If Last Requests Count

The rain will have paused
just long enough
for them to reach the site.
Black suits
and dresses
will turn blacker;
people will slip,
kneeling,
cursing.
The darkness of the clouds
will force sorrow
on the people.
Around the six foot hole,
its mud walls collapsing,
water filling the bottom,
mascara will smear the faces
of these painted clowns.
The men, of course,
will stand stoically
while their own feet
sink deeper
into the soil.
The children
will chase each other
around the gravestones.
The wet rope
and wet hands
will slip
and the box
will fall into the dark,
at an angle.

Two thumps with a shovel
straightens it
and it settles.
"He was a good man…"
the preacher is saying,
but no one hears him,
the sky is exploding.

Construction Worker
Caught in the Rain at Lunch

With rain running
down his rough shirt and jeans
and the water splashing in his boots,
he dripped through the door
of the museum.
He tossed the wet newspaper
he used to cover his head
into a corner
and pulled a rag from his pocket
to wipe mud from his boots.
He pushed his damp hair back
with a large, calloused hand,
held a soggy, brown bag in the other
and stood,
transfixed by Rivera's *American City*.

Tonight I Sleep Alone

Remember Valentine's Day,
a year ago?
I bought a dozen
long-stemmed
red roses
put one on my lapel
and gave you the rest.
Do you remember
the fun we had that evening?
We laughed
and smiled
and talked
and you told me
it had never been better,
never more fun.
And on the way home,
you slept on my shoulder.

Then,
just weeks later,
you left me –
no reason, no explanation.
Everything
I had dreamed of
was destroyed,
nothing left
to rebuild upon.

One year ago –
funny
that it seems so recent.

Once More

A fan sits in the corner
trying to blow away
the humid Houston night.
Rain came
to do its part,
making sounds against the window –
sounds
that can only be described
with clichés.
I lie in bed.
My thoughts
troubled over a girl,
the same problems
every man has:
Problems never solved,
quarrels never settled,
silence taking the place of communication.
The fan moves
from left to right
as I consider
one approach
and then another.
One more night passes
and I fall asleep
with no solutions.

I Remember When

I remember
when I used to come over
and sit on the floor
of your room
and talk.
You'd be in the corner
with your pillows,
and I'd sit across from you,
leaning against your bed.
Face to face,
we'd listen to music
and talk about life.

Now when I come over,
we stay in the living room.
You sit in the recliner
watching television,
and I sit on the couch
trying to break the silence.

A Relationship

My father was in West Texas
taking a picture of an old windmill.
He had climbed onto a fence
to get a different angle
and when he jumped off,
a four-inch Yucca thorn
stuck through one finger
and into his palm
He told me this
and I said,
"Yeah, I bet it did hurt."

I've had splinters and thorns
in my palm before.
Small ones.
They don't always bother me.
I can push that thorn
deeper into my flesh,
where it touches nerves
reminding me I'm alive.
I always hope the thorn will dissolve
and become a part of me.
But sometimes it has to be pulled out
and the deeper I've pushed it,
the more painful it is.

Spring and All

Being spring and all
naturally,
I thought of you.
A long walk
down a dirt road.
Red dust
kicked up by the dog
running in front of us.
Woods on both sides,
a sun peeking through the branches,
a brook hidden by fallen trees,
and vines climbing skyward.
A hand holding a hand
and, softly blowing,
the wind lifts
your blonde hair from your forehead.

The Soldier

I can remember
the first weeks of boot camp:
We rose before the sun
had a chance to wake us
and,
as if feeling cheated,
it beat upon us the rest of the day.
When night came
we were still out there
sweating in the dusty air.
The guys going through their last cycle
used to tell us
we weren't soldiers
until we killed a man.
None of them had ever seen any action,
but we took their word as gospel.

Nobody was tougher
than our drill sergeant.
He said he'd been to Hell and back
and had beaten the devil when he was there.
We believed him.
He told us about Vietnam
and all of the "gooks" he'd killed.
I could see the war
flash in his eyes.

He rode us without pity,
showing no hint
of concern for us.
We used to sit
around the barracks

before lights out
and plot
what we would do to him.

One day,
he caught me behind
the chow hall –
I was skipping duty.
All of a sudden
it was like he was back in Vietnam.
He came after me with death in his eyes.
I caught him on the side of the head
with my rake
and watched as he dropped to his knees,
fell to his face,
and the last memories of Vietnam
slipped away.

I guess now I'm a soldier.

For Terrie

I thought of you
and this is what I wrote:

What will I do
with this handful of minutes
we've spent together?
I will lay them out at home
and relive each one,
savoring them
like morsels of the finest food.
I will replay them.
Watch frame by frame
to catch every nuance
of your smile, eyes
your voice, laugh.
I will listen again and again,
submerged in a flood
of music and emotion.
I will laugh
at being caught up
in something so wonderful,
something I love.
But you will never know
how my heart races
at the thought of you
and then stands still
when we're face to face.
You'll never know that
my throat chokes tight
and my mind goes blank.

That's why I ramble so foolishly.

For William Carlos Williams

I look out my window
and see a lizard
sunning himself
on the ledge.

Serenity

The sun falls behind the mountains.
Its light slips in through the window,
quietly mixing
with the mahogany walls
and leather chairs.

They sit.
He reads a book,
and she, in a brown, woolen sweater,
sips from a warm mug.
The hot chocolate,

its cocoa, sweet
and disarming,
excites her.
He reads on
as she adds wood to the fire.

Her bare feet make no sound
as she moves to sit on the divan.
When he looks up, she smiles
and he sits next to her,
places his hand upon her arm.

She leans toward him,
her shoulder against his,
and curls her legs beneath her.
He sips from her mug,
places his hand on her cheek,
and leans forward.

Their lips touch
but the dog scratches at the door,
a distraction.
When he opens it,
the dog rushes in
and relaxes in front of the fire.

Smoke drifts through the chimney
and into the night.
Geese flying overhead
make shadows
that covers the tracks

of animal chasing animal
in the snow.
The silence of the night
is broken by the echoes
of their cries.

It is warm indoors
and the fires snaps and glints
off the glass-topped table
where the mug
of hot chocolate

sits.

While Fishing

It was while fishing
and looking for more bait
that he found a baby lizard
and thinking
"He will do nicely"
pushed a hook into its stomach
and up through its throat.
The barb came out
right below its chin;
its feet pushed and clawed
at the hook
while its tongue licked at the air.
He cast long, far over the lake,
listening to the ka-plop
as the lizard hit
and sank into the water.
The line twitched the surface
and pulled hard in his hands
and he began reeling in
what turned out to be a 7-pound bass.
He brought it home
in a Styrofoam ice chest
that squeaked on the vinyl seats
each time the car bounced.
Then his wife,
while cleaning the fish,
turned to him and said,
"Look,
    he ate a lizard!"

Security Guard at 2 am

Outside, it is fine and dark,
the guard booth is not well-lighted,
reflections in the window
make it difficult to see
that nothing out of the ordinary
is happening.
The guard looks into the reflections.
He is difficult to see
but that is all right;
no one is looking
and he is not paying attention.
He sits without moving
knowing there is no one to notice
he has drifted to sleep.
The graveyard shift
has taken him
and he is an old man
in the way that old men are
when they are old
and in front of him is a book
of Hemingway
and he says,
"I can not write like this,"
and he is right
and he thinks of going to Harry's
for a drink
and it is a pretty thought.
Outside, it is still fine and dark.

Silence Gives Consent

In the morning
he reaches out his front door
for the newspaper.
He watches his neighbor run by.
Her pristine body
whispers to him
and he draws his bathrobe
tighter.

He wipes breakfast crumbs from his stomach,
sips coffee,
thinks of her.

Lunchtime.
She eats on the patio –
vegetables, bean sprouts,
maybe tofu.
He belches a cheeseburger
and remembers his car needs oil.

From the side of the house,
near the garage,
he sees her sunbathing.
Her suit is untied in the back,
her tan is even, her skin is smooth.

He runs his hand across the dents of his car
and climbs underneath to drain the oil.
He flinches when the oil splatters his hand
realizing he should have let it cool.

He smudges his shirt with oil,
bumps his head on the fender.

The pan of oil sloshes
as he walks to the garage
and looks again at his neighbor.

She doesn't notice
when he walks up to her.
Her eyes are closed
and she doesn't answer
when he asks
if she would like
some oil on her back.

It's A Long Time Until Monday

From the street
he can see her through the window
sitting at her desk.
She holds a pen
tapping a calendar
where she has written for Monday.

He Returns!

It is only Thursday
and the numbers of her clock
glow 9:28
and the radio drips out songs
that go unnoticed.
She plays with the things on her desk,
moving pictures,
rearranging little knick-knacks,
and sometimes standing
and walking to the window
looking out at nothing.
It's only Thursday
and the numbers of her clock
glow 9:29.

One Day Follows the Next

"I throw away the moments of my life
   like unsuccessful poetry,
      tossing them into
         the trashcan of eternity."

Clever thoughts for clever people
he thought
and tossed the book aside.
He always got annoyed
when something he read
seemed to fit his life.
Pushing aside last night's dishes
he kicked his feet up on
the coffee table
to flip through the TV channels.
Nothing interested him anymore.
The floor was a history of the week –
Clothes dumped here and there,
some clean, some dirty,
stacks of books and papers
in constant struggle
against the toppling powers of gravity.
And even as the night approached
and he shed his clothes in a pile
and collapsed onto a bed of crumpled sheets
he thought
   Tomorrow will be different.

M & M

He watches her from across the table –
Her head tilted forward,
her hair shining in the light,
her left hand holding it in place
while she reads his poetry.
Occasionally she laughs –
at a funny line
or at the country music playing around them,
every song about drinking.
He watches her eyes, her face,
as she studies his work.
He watches her cheek dimple when she smiles,
sees her pause at certain times,
knowing she understands.
She turns the pages gently,
she handles his emotions with care.
Her hand touches her cheek,
her chin rests in its palm,
her perfectly curved nails
press into her soft skin.
He wants to reach out,
put his hand there,
tell her she's beautiful.
But there's a little boy
looking over her shoulder.
Maybe he likes poetry
or perhaps he has already developed
an eye for pretty women.

The restaurant is filling now,
people getting louder,
and it gives an excuse to go into the cool night
where they stand close, their breath misting.
She wears a long, white coat
with the collar turned up,
puts her hands in her pockets,
presses her arms tight to her sides
until she's used to the cold.
He puts his arm around her
and they walk down the street
near the old houses.
The sky is clear when they stop.
There's a small park and a bench
so they sit,
close to each other.
They look for constellations
and their laughter warms them
and attracts the attention of people passing by
who whisper.
And they laugh more.
A clock sounds the hour.
It's late,
less people walk by.
It's time to go.
Their walk to the car is slow –
feet, legs moving together,
arms around each other.
Like children, they step over cracks
but give up the game

when cracks overtake the entire sidewalk.
To delay the evening,
he suggests replanting a sprout
that has struggled through the sidewalk,
but the car is waiting.
On the road, after a few minutes,
she is asleep, leaning against him.
The radio plays softly
while she holds his arm and dreams.
He tries not to disturb her
and looks down,
watching the street lamps light up her face.
In this light she is a new beauty.
Asleep
she is free from concern,
her face smooth, relaxed,
and he regrets turning onto her street,
into her drive.
He stops,
turns off the car,
expects her to wake,
but she doesn't.
He puts his arm around her carefully,
and she pulls closer.
He whispers to her,
saying how much fun he had,
how much he loves her,
then looks down to see one eye open,
her lips holding back a grin.
He laughs, kisses her, and walks her to her door.

Turn
off the lights
he said,
hiding under the covers.
She laughed
as
her sockless feet
touched
the stone floor
and he groaned
as she
leapt back into bed,
landing on his stomach.

Go quietly; a dream
when done, should leave no trace
that it has lived, except a gleam
across the dreamer's face.

- Countee Cullen
(1903-1946)

www.ingramcontent.com/pod-product-compliance
Lightning Source LLC
Chambersburg PA
CBHW031321040426
42443CB00005B/170